THE
CAMPER'S
FRIEND

THE CAMPER'S FRIEND

Copyright © Summersdale Publishers Ltd, 2012

Written by Phoebe Smith

Illustrations by Claire Plimmer

Summersdale Publishers Ltd
46 West Street
Chichester
West Sussex
PO19 1RP
UK

www.summersdale.com

Printed and bound in the UK by CPI Group (UK) Ltd, Croydon, CR0 4YY

ISBN: 978-1-84953-248-8

Substantial discounts on bulk quantities of Summersdale books are available to corporations, professional associations and other organisations. For details telephone Summersdale Publishers on (+44-1243-771107), fax (+44-1243-786300) or email (nicky@summersdale.com).

THE
CAMPER'S
FRIEND

A MISCELLANY OF WIT,
WISDOM AND PRACTICAL TIPS

Illustrations by Claire Plimmer

PHOEBE SMITH

summersdale

CONTENTS

INTRODUCTION

*To me a lush carpet of pine needles or
spongy grass is more welcome than
the most luxurious Persian rug.*

HELEN KELLER

I'll never forget the first time I went camping. It was in my best friend's back garden and we were eleven. I remember feeling, though we were only metres from the house, as if we were embarking on a monumental expedition. I remember giggling as our excitement grew when night fell; I remember panicking when, lying in my sleeping bag, I began to ponder the often-asked camping question: 'What if I need the loo?' I recall falling asleep listening to the mysterious sounds of a garden at night and then waking again after what felt like an age, only to realise I'd been out for a mere twenty minutes. But of everything that happened that night, the one bit I remember the most is the feeling I had when I woke up the next morning to find that I had done it. I had survived the night and slept without the comforts of my bedroom. I didn't know it at the time, but some kind of cataclysmic change had occurred in me that morning and things would never be the same again.

Fast-forward another eleven years (and maybe a few more) and my under-canvas experience had exploded – by that point I was hooked. There'd been nights in family campsites, a swag bag under the stars, bivvies, wigwams – you name it, I had tried to sleep in it. But I often wondered if you could ever again experience that unique feeling, that I had back then, of your first ever camp. I began to think not, until a couple of years ago, when I embarked on my first ever solo wild camp.

It was as if I was a child all over again. First came the feeling of a monumental expedition (due mainly to other people's reactions to my chosen quest); my nervous laughter as I mistook a nosey sheep for a potential murderer approaching my tent; my last-minute worry about using 'the facilities' and perhaps the longest night of my life waiting to see if I'd make it till dawn. When I did and I stepped out of my tent into daylight I felt exhilarated – to have spent a couple of days out in the wilderness, with only the outdoor world as company.

It was – and still is – this feeling that causes me to keep heading out on new camping adventures. And I firmly believe it is what drives others to take up the activity.

The fact is that with online social networks, media tablets and MP3 players it's all too easy to lose touch with our world. But camping offers us a brief pause – a breath – to appreciate the much simpler things in life. And to prove we can actually survive with very little indeed.

As you'll soon see, it's what made one Millican Dalton give up his London terrace to live full-time in a tent back in the early 1900s, it's what drove the formation of the oldest camping club in the world and it's what, I hope, made you pick up this book now. So what are we waiting for? Let's kick-start our adventure. Just a quick question – did you pack your sleeping bag? Because I promise this one will be an all-nighter...

Past Tents

With innovation and technology, seems we have forgotten to cherish the true beauty the world has to offer.

A. C. Van Cherub

As long as human beings have existed, the search for shelter – in any form – has, too. We long for somewhere to call home, a place to protect us from the elements and where we can sleep in safety – much like every other animal on the planet. And though over thousands of years we have evolved from the hunter-gatherer days and now live in brick houses rather than in makeshift shelters, garnered from whatever we can find, man has always utilised the tent. Whether it be a temporary home for a wandering tribe, the base for soldiers in military operations or the canvas under which people celebrate a wedding or special occasion, the use of tents definitely has a colourful history. Here are a few noteworthy canvas cocoons from our past...

BEDOUINS, BEDS AND BLISS

A long, long time ago, people lived in nomadic tribes, moving around the land, grazing cattle and setting up home temporarily until the resources ran out, when they simply moved on. These days, permanent dwellings are the order of the day for most of us. However, there are still some nomadic tribes left even in our modern world who live under canvas – or sometimes under the stars with just a mat and sleeping bag. The Bedouins are one such group, who roam parts of North Africa and the Middle East, and still set up camps out in the desert, travelling around regularly, with the only constant being the moon and stars in the sky above their beds – bliss...

HOLIER THAN THOU...

Tents get a mention in the Bible, in the Old Testament. Firstly, in Genesis, we are introduced to Jabel, who is said to be the 'father of all who dwell in tents'; later, in Exodus, Chapter 25, God tells Moses to make him a portable sanctuary (a tabernacle) so that he can dwell with the people. Among his specifications for its design are 'ten curtains of fine twined linen, and blue, and purple, and scarlet', 'fifty taches of gold' to hold the curtains together and 'a covering for the tent of rams' skins dyed red, and a covering above of badgers' skins', as well as tent pegs made of silver. This prestigious-sounding model would certainly have been fitting for a king among kings and its design is what some say the Temple of Solomon in Jerusalem was based on.

This tradition of the ornate tent being used to represent status has continued right through into the modern day. Historically, when royalty or world leaders travelled they would often encamp in gigantic shelters like temporary castles. Think of it as a kind of old-school glamping: Alexander the Great, for example, is said to have had a marriage tent that hung from huge columns of silver and gold.

Go to a campsite today and you're bound to feel a twang of jealousy when your neighbours pull up and erect a huge and luxurious house-like structure, but it makes you feel better to know that tent envy is not a new phenomenon.

WHAT DID THE ROMANS EVER DO FOR US?

During their quest for world domination the Romans were known for erecting huge camps wherever they went, using tents made of leather, big enough to house thousands of their men. But, being Romans, they weren't just put up in a haphazard fashion – these were fancy encampments that boasted streets and a town centre, with lower ranked officers set further away from the middle.

It's not just the power-hungry Romans who have recognised that tents are the perfect way to set up a base quickly in a strategic position – and remove it again equally fast if necessary. Armies have made use of these quick-to-erect structures for millennia, from the Civil Wars in America to World Wars One and Two, and even in Iraq today.

DID YOU KNOW?

There is a tent site in Moldova, Russia that has been tentatively dated back to 40,000 BC. Made of mammoth bones and consisting of the remains of hearths inside, like any temporary structure it is difficult to date with any certainty, but the way it's built, the materials used and the shape of it helps archaeologists to make a good estimate of its age – in this case, the Palaeolithic age.

But the place which you have selected for your camp, though never so rough and grim, begins at once to have its attractions, and becomes a very centre of civilisation to you: home is home, be it never so homely.

HENRY DAVID THOREAU

Anatomy of a Tent

*There's no such thing as bad
weather, just inappropriate gear.*

AN UNKNOWN BUT WISE CAMPER

Cords everywhere, poles to erect, inner and outer sheets, guy lines... What does it all do and what's it for? Let's take a minute to unzip a tent's anatomy once and for all...

Inner and outer sheets – To keep you dry, tents are made up of two layers – the inner and the outer (or flysheet). The inner is the bit that surrounds you when inside it, and even without the outer it's a complete structure with a zippable door that in good quality models is fitted with a midge net to stop bugs getting in. The outer goes over the top of this and also forms a porch at the entrance.

Groundsheet – The part of the tent you lie on, usually made from a robust waterproof fabric as this is what separates you from the ground. Nowadays these are stitched onto the rest of the inner tent and a good one will rise up the sides by several inches. In tepees or larger family tents these are sometimes separate and attach to the main structure of the tent using clips.

Guy lines – These are a set of cords that you peg in to the ground after you've secured the main structure. They work to keep the tent stable in high winds and keep the outer flysheet taut so it doesn't sag and touch the inner tent.

Pegs – Much like tents themselves these come in a range of shapes and sizes. Lightweight wire ones are fine in soft ground and keep your tent weight down, but on harder terrain you'll find durable, thicker pegs more efficient.

Poles – These are vital to form the structure and shape of the tent. Normally these are made of alloy with shock cords running through them so you can dismantle them and fold them up to fit in the stuff sack. They usually fit in sleeves in the tent fabric and lock into eyelets to keep them in place.

Porch – A great place for cooking in high winds or storing dirty boots and wet gear, the porch is sheltered from the elements as it's under the flysheet, but outside the inner tent. It always has a door on it that can be folded back and secured.

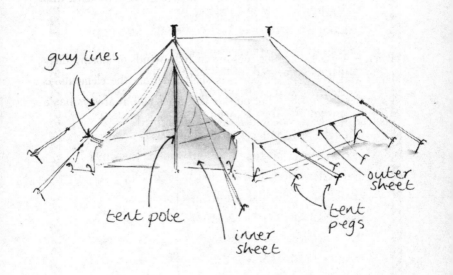

guy lines

tent pole

inner sheet

tent pegs

outer sheet

DID YOU KNOW?

Many people new to camping think their tent is leaking when they wake up after the first night and find the walls dripping wet. Actually, it's just condensation caused by the fact that the air inside the tent is warmer than that outside it. The key to preventing this is good ventilation – gained through mesh panels you'll find on well-designed models – and pitching the tent so that the inner and outer sheets do not touch each other; this allows air to circulate and stops condensation on the underside of the outer soaking through to the inner. You can get single-skin tents (without separate flysheets) but these tend to have real problems with condensation.

So What Kind of Tent Do You Need?

Well, it all depends on what kind of a camper you are. You need to decide a few things before you buy:

How many people is it for?

Tents come in various sizes so check the label to see how many people will sleep in it comfortably. If you plan on doing solo trips, a one-man model will be fine, likewise if you're a couple, a two-man version will do the job, but if you plan to go with friends, or take the kids, you may consider getting one slightly bigger than the number of people going so that you have extra space. Family tents also tend to have separate sleeping quarters so you can give the children a room of their own – also great if you want some privacy.

Will you be wild camping or staying in campsites?
Transporting a tent is definitely something to think about before buying it. If you'll only ever be staying in official campsites and car camping (having your car alongside your tent the whole time), then you can afford to go big and it really doesn't matter how heavy it is. But if you plan on multi-day backpacking trips out in lonely glens or remote moors then every gram will count – so best go for a lighter weight model.

CAMPING MYTH BUSTED:

IF A TENT'S CHEAP, THEN IT WON'T BE ANY GOOD.

Wrong! While it's true that, when it comes to tents, the more you pay the better tent you get – in terms of breathability, durability and performance – that doesn't mean you have to be a millionaire to stay dry and comfortable. Consider how often you'll use it and if it's just once or twice a year, for car camping or in the summer only, then you can easily get away with a lower-end model and still have a great time.

BUYING A TENT – DOS AND DON'TS

Do shop around before buying; you can always find a bargain.

Do make sure you can sit up in your tent comfortably. No headroom means your only option will be lying down – very tedious.

Do pick up the packed tent before you decide – consider if you can manage the weight and whether it will fit in your backpack if necessary.

Don't think that just because a tent packs down into a small bag when you buy it you'll ever be able to fit it back in again after it's been pitched in a rainstorm and you're rushing to put it away with cold hands!

Don't think that just because your friend recommends his or her tent that it will be the right one for you.

Don't buy a tent if the inner and flysheet touch each other when erected.

This Bit Goes Where? – Top Tips for Erecting Your Tent

Putting up a tent can range from relatively easy to harder than constructing a piece of DIY furniture! So, before you head out into the great outdoors there are some things to consider.

Try before you buy – As tents can cost a fair wedge of cash it's certainly not unreasonable to ask the shop assistant for a demo before buying your chosen model. Any good outdoor store will be able to show you the quickest and easiest way to pitch to help you make a decision.

Practice makes perfect – Before you go on your camping trip, it's always a good idea to try putting up your tent at least once in your garden so that it's more familiar (and to check you have all the bits you need!). Much better to struggle with something when there's no audience, pressure or driving rain.

Inner or outer pitch first – Most tents (unless they are for warm weather and so 'single skin') have two layers to them – the inner sheet and the outer sheet. Sometimes you'll find both layers are clipped together so putting it up is done in one go, others pitch the inner first, then the outer (or fly sheet) goes over the top, and finally, some pitch the waterproof outer first then you attach the inner last – to keep it drier. It's best to know which yours is before trying to put it up.

Colourful clues – Poles are often colour-coded so you know which sleeves they fit through and which holes they go into. This can save time when you're pitching in the elements. If they don't come this way, it might be worth colour-coding them yourself.

Don't panic – Struggling with your tent is part of being a camper. Take a deep breath, look at the instructions and try again – shouting has never erected a tent!

A Short History of Camping in Britain

There was the eating tent, the sleeping tent, the servant's tent, the cooking tent for wet weather, and the overboat tent. Here the family and their servants were spending a 'savage' holiday.

Thomas Hiram Holding, *The Camper's Handbook*,
DESCRIBING THE IDEAL CAMPSITE

The practice of going 'back to basics' and camping for the fun of it rather than necessity is relatively new. It all started, in Britain anyway, with one man...

Thomas Hiram Holding (1844–1930)

Though the actual act of sleeping in a tent-like structure was nothing revolutionary a hundred years ago, the idea that you would do it by choice – for fun rather than necessity, and actually enjoy it – was. Thanks to Thomas Hiram Holding, that soon changed.

A tailor by trade, though from a well-off family, his intense love for the great outdoors sprang from an experience he had back in 1853, at the age of nine, when he crossed the American prairies in a wagon train with his parents. He fondly remembered sleeping in the wagon, so once back in the UK he was determined to continue his adventures.

He journeyed to Scotland and travelled and camped in the Highlands with a canoe – an expedition which he wrote about later. He then embarked on a journey across Ireland with four friends, cycling and camping as they went. Such was his love of the trip that on his return he wrote a book about it called *Cycle and Camp in Connemara* and asked readers who would be interested in 'cycle camping' to get in touch with him.

This led to his forming the Association of Cycle Campers in 1901 and after going through various guises this organisation eventually became what is nowadays known as The Camping and Caravanning Club, which boasts over 800 official sites and over 400,000 members.

Holding didn't stop with a club. He went on to write *The Camper's Handbook* in 1908, which, for the first time, gave people a how-to of the basics of sleeping and staying in tents.

Combining his profession as a tailor and hobby as a camper, he also designed some of the first lightweight tents of the time using oiled silk and telescopic poles made from bamboo. He worked on creating a small camping stove that could easily be transported for camping excursions.

Though he is not often mentioned or celebrated, all of us who like nothing more than getting back to nature under our tent – no matter how basic or glam – should remember Thomas and thank him for bringing to us a simple idea that guarantees the adventures never need end.

Camping Collective

During the 1920s and 1930s, with more people pursuing a healthy lifestyle, camping – viewed as an activity that involved large doses of fresh air and was good for you – suddenly experienced a boom in popularity. Car and motorbike ownership was on the up, bringing with it the opportunity to escape from day-to-day life, and people soon realised that if you threw a tent into the mix you could get extended time away.

Reflecting its popularity, by 1932, with a bulging membership, The Camping and Caravanning Club formed the International Federation of Camping Clubs (Fédération Internationale de Camping et de Caravanning, FICC), which meant other national camping clubs worldwide would be affiliated with them, creating a truly global network of opportunities to camp out – with access to some exclusive members only sites and discounted rates to all the others.

On Fame's eternal camping-ground
Their silent tents are spread,
And Glory guards with solemn round
The bivouac of the dead.

THEODORE O'HARA

The War Years

The advent of World War One had an oddly positive effect on camping. Soldiers became accustomed to living in very basic conditions, and though sadly many never returned from the battlefield, some of those who did got a taste for travelling and seeing the world from a tent. The amount of army surplus kit that became available once the war was over meant even more people could afford to give it a go, boosting its appeal.

During World War Two, people were keen to get out of major towns and cities and into the safer environment of the countryside, and in 1941 the Youth Camping Association was formed. And when the war was over, families began to indulge in cheap camping holidays using army surplus gear once more.

In the 1950s, following Sir Edmund Hilary's conquest of Everest, public interest in adventure soared, putting camping firmly on the map.

The Swinging Sixties

It wasn't just ideals that changed in the 1960s – camping got a makeover, too. Rather than just khaki army surplus tents, colourful models arrived on the scene. Fabric makers who had concentrated all their efforts on war materials now began to design and experiment in other areas. Among them was entrepreneur Robert Saunders, who created a lightweight tent out of nylon. Kit had become good quality and affordable. Families now had paid holiday time from work and more had cars, and more official campsites sprung up all over the UK offering extra amenities and facilities. Soon camping was the most popular kind of holiday. This very British love affair with the tent was mirrored in the classic 1969 movie *Carry On Camping*, starring Sid James and Barbara Windsor.

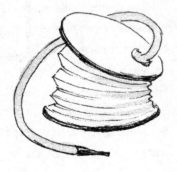

THE LURE OF ABROAD?

In the 1970s and 1980s, the availability of cheap package holidays to destinations guaranteeing sunshine during precious time off work meant the UK camping holiday was, unsurprisingly, abandoned by many in favour of a week of sun, sea and sand in foreign climes. However, there were still many stalwart outdoor lovers who would combine the two – taking their tents overseas for camping holidays, European style. And with music festivals increasing in popularity the convenience of tent-side adventure was not forgotten.

Good thing too, as the early 1980s saw a recession pricing many families out of flying off on package holidays. Britain began camping once more, for very little money at all.

More recently, the 1990s and 2000s saw increasing concern about the environmental impact of air travel, meaning many opted to rediscover the beautiful landscapes of the UK for their vacations. The continuing growth in popularity of outdoor music festivals coupled with another recession have helped revive people's love of what is a cheap and cheerful way to vacation. With innovative designs and brand new fabrics making camping more of a luxury affair, the Brits are falling in love with camping in Britain all over again. The staycation is here and long may it reign – though hopefully not rain!

TENT TYPES

*Whatever special nests we make – leaves
and moss like the marmots and birds,
or tents or piled stone – we all dwell
in a house of one room – the world
with the firmament for its roof.*

JOHN MUIR

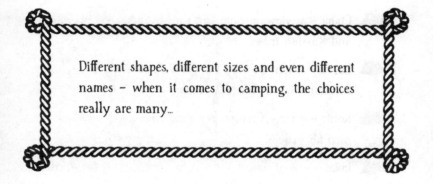

Different shapes, different sizes and even different names – when it comes to camping, the choices really are many...

A TENT BY ANY OTHER NAME...

Thought it was just called a tent and that was it? Your pack-away home from home comes in many other guises and has many different names around the globe – see which ones you've heard of:

- **Wigwam** – a dome structure used by Native American tribes.

- **Chum** – a wigwam-type tent used by nomadic Siberian and Russian tribes.

- **Lavvu** – a tent used by the Sami of northern Scandinavia, similar to a Chum.

- **Kohte** – a large German Scouting tent, typically black, used for groups.

- **Loue** – a very simple, ultra-light Finnish tent designed for one or two people.

- **Pandal** – a type of fabric structure constructed for religious ceremonies in Asia.

- **Sibley** – a conical tent designed for use by the US Army in 1856.

- **Yurt** – a wooden frame temporary tent structure used by Turks in Central Asia.

WHAT, NO CANVAS?

Though the traditional material associated with tents is this 100 per cent cotton fabric, and we still use the nostalgic expression 'sleeping under canvas', it actually hasn't been used in modern tent manufacturing for decades. It's undoubtedly a breathable fabric – being less prone to condensation building up inside – and can be coated to make it waterproof, but it lost favour with campers because of its weight compared to modern-day man-made fabrics such as nylon, PVC and polyester.

What Kind of Tent?

When it comes to your portable home there are literally hundreds of makes, styles, fabrics and sizes to choose from, but despite all the colours and brands that scream at you when you walk into a gear shop, tents can roughly be divided into five categories:

A-frame – If you asked a child to draw a tent, chances are they would draw one that looked like this. Based on the original canvas tent, A-frames use two sloping upright poles at each end that meet at the top to create the triangular shape and usually a connecting ridge pole along the roof, which makes for a very stable structure. This is the classic design of tents but in recent years A-frames have waned in popularity due to the amount of internal space lost by the sloping side walls when compared to other models.

Tunnel tents – A popular design that relies on traction to help create and maintain its tunnel shape, which you make when pegging it out. Due to the hooped structure you usually get quite a lot of space inside, meaning you can sit up with no problem. As some one- and two-person designs use only one central hoop/pole these are often a popular option for lightweight enthusiasts. The only drawback can be the flatter roof shape they inevitably form that can collect heavy rain or snow and make them sag

Geodesic tents – Invented after World War One and sometimes known as dome tents, the main feature of this structure is that once the poles are in place the tent is freestanding, meaning you can move it once it's up and simply peg it in place to hold it down. The advantage, of course, is its stability once erected. This has made it one of the most popular designs for use on modern-day expeditions.

Box tents – Head to any popular campsite this summer and chances are you will see a field of large family tents based on this design. Thanks to their height and shape (literally a large rectangular box) they offer an abundance of headroom, meaning you can stand up and walk around in them as if at home. As they are built for comfort they usually consist of several 'rooms' but because of this they are quite heavy. A perfect solution for large groups on extended stays when camping from your car.

Conical tents – These single pole supported designs – think tepee or bell tent – have been used for centuries by indigenous nomadic people such as the Native Americans and Sami tribes. The style was even adopted by explorer Ernest Shackleton on his polar expedition in 1914. The simple pitch system allows shelter to be created quickly and the cone shape means a low centre of gravity that keeps the tent stable in wind and leaves plenty of space in the centre, traditionally used for a fire to warm the living space.

DON WHILLANS (1933-85)

Better known as a climber and adventurer than a camper, the Mancunian legend who was Don Whillans is also renowned to those in the gear industry for brainstorming several designs that had and continue to have influence on the kit that we still see around today.

Whillans had many achievements to his name, not least that he brought the formerly rich man's game of mountaineering to the working classes with a determined attitude and straight-talking manner. Within his lifetime he made the first ascent of the mighty south face of Annapurna (with Dougal Haston) – one of the most significant British mountaineering achievements of the past fifty years. He also scaled unclimbed routes on Mont

Blanc, making him something of a celebrity, and completed a successful first ascent of the Central Tower of Paine in Patagonia.

As well as having a natural skill on rock, he also had a real interest in kit, always trying to think of ways to make the gear he was using more fit for purpose. It was while climbing in 1963 that he designed and constructed what is commonly referred to as the 'Whillans Box'. Rectangular and cumbersome looking, this tent actually played a crucial role in his success in Patagonia. Though it looked odd next to the more modern dome tents on the same trip used by other mountaineers, the weather conditions destroyed those conventional mountain tents, while his design stood up to everything nature threw at it. With a sturdy construction designed to withstand an avalanche, it became something of a trademark on many of the expeditions led by Sir Chris Bonington in the 1970s on both Everest and Annapurna. Mike Parsons of Karrimor tweaked the design using aluminium poles to strengthen it further while keeping it light, but sadly it never did quite catch on in its Whillans guise as a consumer product.

Following a much publicised battle with booze and a string of run-ins with the law, Whillans sadly died of a major heart attack in his sleep. His amazing climbing talent and quick wit is still remembered fondly and campers should thank him: his design clearly became the inspiration for many of the large family tents still used today. Don Whillans – we salute you!

PITCH PERFECT

*The real enjoyment of camping and tramping
in the woods lies in a return to primitive
conditions of lodging, dress, and food, in
as total an escape as may be from the
requirements of civilisation. It is wonderful to
see how easily the restraints of society fall off.*

CHARLES DUDLEY WARNER, 'CAMPING OUT'

So, you've got your tent, packed all your goodies and rocked up at your chosen campsite – but where to pitch? There will be times when you don't have a choice, but if you do...

SCOPE OUT A GOOD SITE

Location, location – There are different things to consider when picking where to base yourself. For example, being close to the toilets and water facilities might be handy if you need to go in the night, but bear in mind you'll probably be disturbed by other people making a visit there.

When the wind blows – High winds can not only make your tent fabric flap and keep you up at night, but can also loosen guy lines, meaning you have to keep getting out and readjusting them – not fun. Position your tent so that the sharpest bit faces the wind, to break it, and if possible keep your entrance away from the prevailing wind.

Things that go bump in the night – You won't get a good night's sleep if you end up on uneven ground, so before you position the tent, lie down on the ground to check it's comfortable and free of hidden holes, lumps and bumps or big rocks. You will rarely get a completely flat piece of ground to pitch on but remember on a slope – even a slight one – it's more comfortable to keep your head uphill and your feet downhill, especially if there's more than one of you. You don't want to find yourselves sliding out of bed sideways and ending up in a heap at one end of the tent!

Keep it steady – When pegging out your tent position the guy lines into the wind and try to get a 90-degree angle between them and the pegs.

Everybody needs good neighbours – Have a look at the other people you'll be sleeping next to – if they are there to have a late night and you are an early riser, or you're there for peace and quiet and they have lots of children, then you may want to consider choosing another spot.

Camping: the art of getting closer to nature while getting farther away from the nearest cold beverage, hot shower and flush toilet.

ANONYMOUS

DEALING WITH DIFFICULT GROUND

Once you've picked your spot, pitching a tent should be a relatively straightforward affair, but what happens if you encounter a site with tricky ground? Fear not, there are some ways around it:

Problem: Can't get your pegs in the ground
Solution: Rocks can make good anchor points as an alternative. If they are small, loop your guy lines and cords around them then wedge a much heavier rock on top to act as the anchor.

Problem: The ground is too rocky
Solution: Look for cracks on large slabs of rock – you may be able to hammer your pegs into those and wedge them in position.

Problem: It's too windy so your tent keeps lifting up
Solution: Place your gear at the four corners of your tent to weigh it down. If that's a problem because your bag isn't heavy enough, use some rocks instead.

Problem: Your guy lines need to stretch further
Solution: Look for cord that you can use to extend them – perhaps the draw cord on your sleeping bag's stuff sack or rucksack.

WEIRD BUT WONDERFUL

By far the oddest campsite to pitch at has to be Hertshoon in the Netherlands. Here you'll be surrounded by the usual campsite trappings – toilet and shower block, amenity shop and green grass – but additionally you'll notice that several of your fellow campers will be settled into tents not on the ground but dangling in the trees. These huge green canvas structures float from the branches like giant teardrops – though definitely the happy kind! Inside they support two semi-circular camping mats and next to the entrances there are picnic tables on stilts where you can cook your dinner without having to descend from your tent. Using one of these certainly takes pitching a tent to the next level – though at least it removes the worry of uneven ground. Thankfully, you don't have to worry about pitching it yourself. To find out more about these tree dangling designs see www.ardoer.com.

Wild Camping

I would rather wake up in the middle of nowhere than in any city on earth.

Steve McQueen

Campsites are great. You get flushing toilets, hot showers, a place to park the car and sometimes even a shop to buy your supplies. They're convenient, they're friendly, but... here's the thing: everyone knows where they are. Camping is supposed to be about enjoying the outdoors and getting back to the simple life, surrounded by nature, but that's pretty hard to do when to even get to your tent you have to negotiate a family game of rounders and trip over a rambunctious dog, and then fall asleep to your neighbours' snoring.

So how do you enjoy all the best of camping with none of the people? The answer is wild camping. The premise is simple: choose your area, pack your tent and head into the landscape, map in hand for a night (or several) out under the stars. No campsites, no other people, no problems.

IS IT LEGAL?

There's a real history of mountaineers and walkers sleeping in the UK hills and, thanks to the Land Reform Act 2003, in Scotland wild camping (done properly – see below) is still perfectly legal. That's also the case in Dartmoor, where the right to wild camp falls under the National Parks and Access to the Countryside Act 1949. Elsewhere you're supposed to ask the landowner's permission before sleeping on their land, but it is usually tolerated provided you remain discreet and follow the basic wild camp etiquette.

WILD CAMP ETIQUETTE

Arrive late and leave early – Plan to arrive at your chosen location as it's going dark and be packed up and away by the time other walkers are out and about.

Never light an open fire – A lot of places suitable for wild camping present a high risk of fire so never do this; you don't want to be responsible for destroying acres of beautiful landscape and devastating ecosystems!

Leave no trace of your camp – Make sure you carry out your rubbish; you should leave the site as you found it.

Be considerate of others – Respect the privacy and livelihood of others; if asked to move on, do so, and keep away from main tracks and paths.

Camp high – Stay on ground that's well away from people's property and keep it discreet and you should have no problems.

Choose your toilet carefully – Find a sheltered spot at least 50 metres away from water and downstream of popular camping areas. Dig a 6–8-inch deep hole, and replace the earth once you have finished your business. Remember to carry out your toilet roll with your other rubbish.

WHERE TO GO...

If it's your first time, you'll sleep a lot more soundly doing it somewhere you know it's legally allowed:

Dartmoor

Nestled in the wilds of south Devon, in the south-west of England, this vast and rough granite moorland offers endless possibilities for wild camping and exploration. It's famous for its weather shaped tors – rocky boulder-like outcrops that stud the hilltops and attract peregrine falcons, which add an atmospheric air to the place – and is laced with snaking rivers cutting dramatically through the landscape. Thanks to its geographical location the weather here tends to be better than other high places in the UK and you can camp in most places within the park – it's a case of grabbing your map and plotting your route. But a great option is to head north from Ivybridge. En route you can check out the longest known stone row in the world on Erme Plains before heading to Higher Hartor Tor for stunning views and a possible night out under the stars. For tips on where to camp, any seasonal restrictions and military firing times check out www.dartmoor.npa.gov.uk.

Scotland

With so much stunning scenery to choose from throughout the country, no matter where you go you're sure to have a memorable evening. The Southern Uplands – including the tarns (small mountain lakes) around the highest peak, the Merrick – are great for stargazing, being the place in the UK furthest from light pollution. The mountains around Glen Coe are steeped in legend and history – from the pyramidal Buachaille Etive Mòr to the Lost Valley, they are a perfect place to bed down surrounded by soaring peaks. Or you could choose a beach like Sandwood Bay in the far north – it's over a mile long and has no road access and its golden sand dunes offer a multitude of pitching opportunities – and if you're lucky you might even spot the Northern Lights.

BEFORE YOU GO

It's good to scope out your potential pitch first by looking on a map before you leave home so at least you have somewhere to aim for. Here's what to look out for on an OS Explorer map (1:25,000):

Green slashes – These indicate a bog, and as well as spelling a soggy night for you they can also mean midges, so avoid them.

Blue lines – These show rivers (or blue patches for larger tarns/lakes); being close to one is always handy to source water for cooking and drinking, meaning you don't have to carry in much, though you should always boil water first.

Broken lines – These indicate paths and tracks. Wild camping is tolerated as long as people are discreet, so avoid these to make sure you stay out of sight.

Wobbly black clusters – These indicate the curves of corries or crags. Look for patterns of these that form a C-shape, which will shield you from high wind.

Is It Safe?

Compared to walking at night in any big city, wild camping is perfectly safe. I have done it myself many times, even on my own, and never experienced any problems. Take the usual precautions of telling someone what you're doing, where you're going and when you should be back, but there's no need to worry. Have fun and enjoy the experience! If you don't feel happy about it, head home: it's supposed to be for pleasure – not a challenge.

YOU KNOW YOU'RE A
WILD CAMPER WHEN...

... someone has to politely point you to the toilet block when you start to dig a hole to 'do your business'.

YOU SHOULD STICK
TO CAMPSITES IF...

... your idea of camping is taking a four-man tent, flocked air mattress and a double-hob cooker – even when camping alone.

FAR FROM THE MADDING CROWD

*I suspect that many of us are, after all, really
camping temporarily in civilised conditions;
and that going into the wilderness is an escape,
longed for, into our natural and preferred state.*

CHARLES DUDLEY WARNER, *IN THE WILDERNESS*

'Sometimes you have to come out here and get away from it all. To take only what you need to survive and be close with this world.'

So a Bedouin once told me when I was camping out in Wadi Rum – a vast expanse of desert plains, punctuated with huge scoured rocky peaks, stretching on for miles in the south of Jordan. Though his people were historically nomadic, he, like many of them, had a family home in a village. But despite having all the creature comforts of our modern world at his disposal, he explained how he often felt the urge simply to head out into the emptiness of the desert – a place that can be harsh even for those who know it well.

He, of course, was onto something. There is no better escape from our fast-paced society than heading into the wilderness, tent in hand, and reconnecting with a world with which we can all too often feel we've lost touch.

The fact is that humans have always had a strong connection to nature; when in the outdoors, the feel, smells, sights and sounds can stir something very primal in us. Though our caves and mud huts have morphed into concrete apartments and brick semi-detached houses, our need to experience the call of the wild, even just now and again, is something that we'll probably never lose and that is why camping is so important. Not only is it fun: it's good for you.

There is a serene and settled majesty to woodland scenery that enters into the soul and delights and elevates it, and fills it with noble inclinations.

WASHINGTON IRVING

LORD AND LADY BADEN-POWELL (1857–1941 AND 1889–1977)

Forefather of the Scouting movement, Robert Baden-Powell created an organisation which, to this day, teaches young people the joys of reconnecting with the outdoors. It all started when he returned from war with the idea that youths, like soldiers, could be taught useful skills in the wilderness to prepare them for life. In 1907 he took twenty-one boys (roughly between the ages of nine and fifteen) camping on a trip to Brownsea Island to see how his ideas would work. This was hugely successful and he went on to write a book that covered essential knowledge like tracking, signalling, camping and cooking.

The organisation grew in popularity and in 1909 girls began to ask why they couldn't learn these skills and go camping. Robert decided to take action – a revolutionary step back then, when girls even going hiking was seen as a bit of a social taboo. And so in 1910 the Girl Guides was launched so that they, too, could get out there and feel at home in the outdoors.

Soon, learning bushcraft and camping was an international obsession and in 1918 Robert's wife Olave became the chief guide for Britain (and the world chief guide in 1930). She actively encouraged women to get involved with guiding, and after her husband died she continued to fly the flag for Scouting and camping, which ensured a new generation of outdoor lovers after the war.

Their legacy and love for camping and wilderness training survives today, with worldwide Scouting membership in the millions.

TOP FIVE THINGS ABOUT CAMPING

Freedom – Want a quick escape to the countryside? A night out on a beach? A weekend of waking up surrounded by mountains? With camping, you can go anywhere you want with very little pre-planning.

Peace and quiet – Camping really gives us the chance to pause in our busy lives and literally smell the roses.

It's cheap – For as little as £5 a night you can wake up in the type of surrounds that money quite simply can't buy.

Learning to appreciate the little things – Making a brew in your kitchen is never cause for celebration but when you're camping the satisfaction you'll get boiling up a hot drink on a stove is unbelievable.

Coming back home again – Because nothing will make you appreciate all mod cons, solid walls and real mattresses like a camping trip!

GWEN MOFFAT (1924-)

Back in the 1940s, despite the wartime efforts seeing women breaking out of the home and taking on less traditional roles, the climbing world was still definitely a male-dominated one. But one woman, called Gwen Moffat, challenged this. Working as a driver in the Auxiliary Territorial Service through World War Two she found herself drawn to the mountains.

Post conflict in 1946, when driving in Wales she met a conscientious objector whose tales of adventure involving rock-climbing and countryside bivvies convinced her that she should pursue her passion. She went AWOL from the army and would hitchhike her way around the country, sleeping in tents, dossing in derelict hillside cottages to perfect her sport. Chances are if you had gone to north Wales any time in the late 1940s and early 1950s you might have seen Gwen either climbing barefoot on some gnarly looking crag or roughing it, camping under a hedge.

She didn't care what anyone thought of her; she just headed out into the wilds to be surrounded by the rocks that she adored. Her love of the outdoors was a habit that she simply couldn't break and after years of pursuing her passion in 1953 she became the first ever female mountain guide – even by the 1990s there were only four women who had achieved this. Her ability and rope work put her well up there with her male peers and she went to the Alps and Scotland on many expeditions as 'one of the boys' to push her skills to new heights.

Though she toned down her canvas nights as she got older and forged a successful career as a crime writer, she never truly left the wilderness and mountainscapes that she loved, weaving them into her books.

Had it not been for her breaking out from the traditional woman's place in the home it might have been much longer before other women followed in her footsteps and tried their hand at climbing, and until women and men took part in base camp missions together to climb some of the world's highest mountains.

Thanks to her, many women were inspired to pitch a tent far from the madding crowd and truly get away from it all – and experience that addictive quality that hooked Gwen. Really, Ms Moffat, you have a lot to answer for...

Want to know more about the elusive Ms Moffat? Check out her autobiography *Space Below My Feet* (Sigma, 2001).

IN THE BAG

*If one way be better than another, that
you may be sure is Nature's way.*

ARISTOTLE

Camping is about getting back to nature, so be sensible when packing. If wild camping, take only the essentials; if staying on a campsite, you can take a few more creature comforts.

Sleeping mat – Whether you want the luxury of a flocked mattress (remember the pump if required!), a metal-framed camp bed, a self-inflating lightweight number or a traditional closed-cell foam mat, you'll need something to insulate you from the ground.

Sleeping bag – Down or synthetic, the choice is yours. Though it depends on a number of factors (including loft factor and fill level), down is sometimes lighter for the same level of warmth as some synthetics but if you get it wet/damp it won't work properly so think about the conditions you'll experience and check the temperature ratings when buying to make sure you'll stay warm enough.

Sleeping bag liner (optional) – This can not only keep you warmer, but also delay the need to wash your sleeping bag, extending its life.

Pillow (optional) – A pillow can make the difference between a good and a great night's sleep so it's worth considering. If car camping, you can take a normal pillow, but if wild camping consider an inflatable model or simply make one using a dry bag stuffed with a warm jacket.

Stove – There's a choice of lightweight and luxury to fit your purpose, but remember to take matches or a lighter, and you'll need fuel, too.

Cooking pot/mess tin – For heating food and water.

Crockery and utensils – You'll need a mug, plate/bowl, cutlery and cooking utensils (see camp cooking section for detailed list).

Washing-up kit – A small bowl, detergent and a sponge can really help keep the mess down to a minimum.

Water container – Even if you're on a campsite, you don't want to keep going back and forth to the tap, so take a large plastic holder.

Head torch – You can take regular torches or lanterns for illuminating the inside of your tent, but the advantage of a head torch is that you get to keep both hands free, making it ideal when cooking.

Towel – A small, quick-dry one is always useful for your hands; just don't forget you'll need a separate (larger) one for the showers.

Wash bag – Just because you're roughing it doesn't mean you won't want to keep clean. A small bag with all your toiletries in it will come in handy – you can pick it up before heading to the shower block without forgetting anything.

Camera – These are the days you'll want to remember so best pack one of these to capture some treasured memories.

Duct tape – A great accessory that fixes a multitude of sins!

Dry bags (optional) – Often sold in packs of several different colours and sizes, these are a great way to organise your kit and keep anything important away from condensation.

Warm layer – As the sun sets you will get colder even if it's summer; make sure you take a warm jacket to put over your other clothes so you don't have to go straight to bed when the sun sets.

Rucksack – If you're wild camping/backpacking you'll need to make sure your backpack is big enough for purpose. A 50-litre bag is usually sufficient.

TREAT YOURSELF...

You're out there to enjoy nature, not simply survive in it, so don't be afraid to pack a little treat. Whether it's a bottle of wine, a good book, a cake or a coffee maker it never hurts to bring something to make you smile!

Packing Your Rucksack

Heading off into the hills for an extended walk and camp? Here's how best to pack your bag.

Tent – This is usually the biggest and bulkiest item you'll carry. It is easily stored attached to the outside of your rucksack in a waterproof stuff sack (usually at the bottom using straps).

Heavy items – Items such as sleeping bag, mat and stove should be positioned as close to your centre of gravity as possible: so in the middle of your bag, near to your back.

Light items – Maps, compass, snacks, etc. can be further away from your centre of gravity, so an outer pocket will be fine.

Fuel canisters – Store them upright and on the outside of your pack if possible.

Waterproofs – Keep these close to hand at the top of your rucksack, so you can grab them quickly if the weather suddenly turns.

CAMPING
WITHOUT CANVAS

The person with the fewest
possessions is the freest.

PAUL THEROUX, *THE HAPPY ISLES OF OCEANIA*

Despite the fact that, for some, a night out under canvas (or, more commonly, waterproof nylon) is an adventure already, there are others who see sleeping in a tent as a bit too – dare we say it – tame. And if you've ever tried sleeping out in the open, with nothing but the stars for a roof – even just in your own back garden – you'll see that it's an unrivalled way of getting close to nature. So if you're feeling like a change from the ordinary, why not shun the tent and give one of these a go?

CAVES

Thanks to millennia of glacial erosion our landscape has been scoured into a huge network of nooks and crannies, with cathedrals of rock carved into mountainsides that are just begging to be explored. Due to their dark corners and sometimes unknown depths, these crevices tend to get something of a mythical reputation. A case in point is the secret cave on Moel yr Ogof in Snowdonia, north Wales. The story goes that when Owain Glyndwr – the self-declared prince of Wales – was being pursued by the invading English, he clambered into this small crack and hid out. His would-be attackers tried to follow him but to reach it involved a scramble on loose rock and after several of them fell they gave up.

Nowadays there are several known caves, shelter stones, and howfs (overhanging rocks) peppered around the UK that adventure seekers regularly sleep in – some even have a book in which you can record your visit!

TOP TIPS FOR A CAVE SLEEP

Do your research before you go. You want a cave that is in a safe condition – no rocks balancing precariously above you or risk of flooding.

Bigger isn't better. For the purposes of a camp-out in a cave you want a small and shallow opening that is easy to get in and out of should you need to make a sharp exit.

You will get wet. Though, in theory, sleeping in a cave means you're given natural shelter, there are very few 'dry' caves, so take a waterproof bag to put your sleeping bag in, i.e. a bivvy bag.

Respect your surroundings – you want to make sure that the cave is there for future campers to enjoy, so make sure you take out all your rubbish and leave it in the same condition you found it.

TARP

Before tents became super light, the tarp – a simple sheet of waterproof fabric that you can stretch out between trees, stones or walking poles – was the connoisseur's choice for a weight-friendly alternative. The past few years have seen one-man tunnel tents becoming so light that the tarp has lost its edge, though there are still some 'get-back-to-basics' nature-loving aficionados who continue to use them. With these you literally do get close to nature because – in dry conditions – you can sleep with no groundsheet between you and the ground and no fabric walls around you. If you want to watch a sunrise from a summit or sleep out in the woods, then under a tarp is the ultimate way to do it.

BIVVY BAG

Sometimes used as an emergency option by climbers caught out in the Alps, these waterproof sacks lie somewhere in the middle ground between tent and tarp, being not quite as light as a simple fabric sheet, but not nearly as roomy as a full-on tent.

Only big enough for you, your sleeping mat and sleeping bag (everything else needs to stay outside), they usually have a hoop near the head and some of the posh ones have a flysheet so that you can leave the door open to stare at the stars – and to stop you feeling like you're in a body bag. They can be a great way to lighten your kit and you'll find you can tuck them in to some cracking spots and watch the day melt into night while you're snuggled in your bivvy.

Remember to take waterproof bags for your kit when bivvying as you won't fit it in with you and no one wants to put on wet clothes if it rains overnight.

BOTHY

For those who have never had the fortune to have slept in one, the idea of a bothy – a house-like structure in the middle of some of the most dramatic mountains in the country that you can sleep in for free – can sound far-fetched. And indeed it is almost too good to be true. But it's something that's been going on since the end of World War Two, when mountaineering's popularity increased and hill farming was on the decline, leaving buildings abandoned in really wild and remote areas.

Thanks to the Mountain Bothies Association (MBA) – a volunteer-run organisation – more than a hundred of these otherwise dilapidated shelters across the country have been lovingly restored and maintained, making staying out in the mountains tent-free a much easier prospect.

Ranging from simple shelters with nothing more than four walls, a roof and a shovel for 'toilet duties', to those with running water and a flushing loo, bothies are the perfect way to experience a real taste of the outdoors without your canvas shelter. Long live the MBA!

Know the Bothy Code

Bothies are a blessing so make sure you do your bit to help keep them that way.

Take rubbish with you – Litter breeds more litter so any you take with you (even if it's not yours) will help keep it clean.

Use the shovel – When there's no toilet make sure you bury all your waste well away from the water supply and the bothy itself.

Make friends – Bothies are all about socialising so make any other visitors welcome; remember it's there for you to share.

Check the date – Some bothies sit within areas used for deer stalking so check with the estate before you go to make sure access isn't closed.

For the MBA's Bothy Code, to donate or to volunteer to help maintain a bothy, see www.mountainbothies.org.uk.

THE CAMP KITCHEN

How come one match can start a forest fire,
but it takes a whole box to start a campfire?

CHRISTY WHITEHEAD

Heading into the outdoors on a camping trip can take you right back to a much simpler way of life. And everyone knows in a time when man didn't have to worry about modern technology there were two concerns: sleeping and... eating. One of the most important elements of camping is food and – here's the thing – it's not all Pot Noodles!

WHAT TO PACK IN THE KITCHEN SACK

While you obviously can't and shouldn't take your whole kitchen with you, it doesn't mean that you have to compromise on great meals. It's all down to the right equipment.

If staying on a campsite (as opposed to wild camping), don't leave home without:

- Stove
- Fuel – make sure it's the right kind for your stove
- Cutlery
- Plates/bowls
- Mug
- Frying pan
- Saucepan
- Wooden spoon
- Tongs
- Sharp knife
- Chopping board
- Scissors
- Bottle/can opener

STOVES OR BBQ?

When it comes to cooking outdoors there are several options available:

Luxury stove – Need twin hobs? Want the option of a grill? Staying in a proper campsite? Then this is the model for you. Basically a slimmed-down version of a cooker you might have at home, this is great for doing more ambitious meals where you'll need to have two pans on the go and want more versatility. They are obviously heavy, so not suitable for backpacking or wild camping, and can run off a number of fuel systems (see page 96).

Backpacking stove – There are a multitude of brands to choose from, and all use the same principle: a small burner and pan stand that tends to have an inbuilt lighter (do check before abandoning your lighter/matches, though!) which fits straight onto a gas canister. These are best for boiling water and cooking camping meals and, as they're usually lightweight, are obviously great for wild camping trips.

Solid fuel burning stoves – Epitomised by the Kelly Kettle, these devices rely on you gathering your own fuel, be it wood, newspaper or dry leaves, which you load in the bottom then cook on the top – very environmentally friendly.

BBQ – Whether you buy a disposable version or stick to the reusable charcoal model, in the summer these can be a great choice for outdoor cooking.

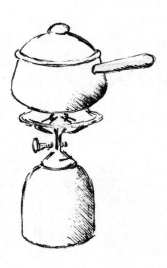

FUEL FOR THOUGHT

Camping stoves use several types of fuel, including:

Gas – This is usually a propane/butane mix in pressurised canisters that are widely available to buy from outdoor shops. Before buying a refill, check whether your stove is a screw-on type or the sort which requires you to pierce the canister.

Methylated spirit – Easy and safe to use, as it is unpressurised, but not as readily available. It can also be slower to burn.

Paraffin – This burns under pressure but needs a liquid like petrol or meths to prime the stove – smells strong.

Petrol/diesel – This is cheap but can be dirty and smelly to use.

SMELL SOMETHING?

R emember that when campsite cooking you need to be careful.

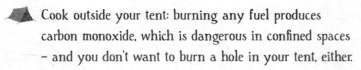

Cook outside your tent: burning any fuel produces carbon monoxide, which is dangerous in confined spaces – and you don't want to burn a hole in your tent, either.

Ensure you place your stove on a flat surface so it doesn't fall over.

Never leave your stove unattended – it's easy for something to boil over quickly and then it can be difficult to reach the off switch.

Check that you've turned the gas all the way off when you've finished cooking.

GRAB SOME GRUB

When going on long backpacking trips or wild camping you might not feel like carting around lots of ingredients; that's when prepared meals come into their own. You have two choices:

Dehydrated meals – Dried food that you simply add boiling water to and leave for several minutes before digging in. Very lightweight but... if your stove isn't working or you can't source water, you will go hungry.

Boil in the bag – A heavier option, but in this packet all the food is pre-cooked and simply needs heating up; the advantage with these is that in an emergency you can resort to eating the contents cold.

PIMP YOUR PACKET!

Jazzing up your camping meals is easy, simply by taking any of these lightweight ingredients in your rucksack:

- Sundried tomatoes
- Paprika
- Cumin
- Raisins
- Couscous

CAMPERS' RAISIN BREAD

G reat for breakfast, as a side to a camp meal or a simple snack.

Ingredients:

- Knob of butter or small amount of cooking oil (for greasing your pan)
- 400 g self-raising bread flour
- Handful of raisins
- 7 tbsp powdered milk
- 2 tsp baking powder
- 1 tsp salt

1. Mix everything together in a bowl/mess tin.

2. Add cold water until the consistency is sticky.

3. Lightly oil your pan with butter or oil and lay your dough into it so it forms a layer about 1 centimetre in thickness.

4. Heat gently, continuously turning over. It will rise as you heat it.

5. Serve when nicely browned on both sides. Add sugar or butter to taste.

STORE IT

Outdoor living means you have to think carefully about where to keep your tasty loot.

Plastic containers should be used to keep the food fresh and to stop wildlife eating your food – though bear in mind keeping it in the car may be the best way to keep a determined badger out! Remember to pack these so you can put any dry food in them when you've finished cooking.

Cool boxes are great for keeping things nice and icy but remember that leaving food items carefully positioned in a shallow stream (heavier items only, to stop them being carried away by the current) or even just outside in colder temperatures will work just as well.

Bushcraft Basics

The great thing about bushcraft is that wherever you go, the skills go with you.

Ray Mears

Think bushcraft is all about eating rotting animal carcasses? Think again. It's really about utilising nature's bounty to enhance your outdoor experience. So while out camping, why not try one of these traditional techniques?

Raid Nature's Pantry

Classically, when we think of wild food we think mushrooms and fungi. However, given the difficulties in identifying non-poisonous types, it's a case of 'If you're not 100 per cent sure, leave it!'. But 'shrooms aside, there are lots of other naturally found foods that are easy to identify and tasty enough to enliven any camping kitchen.

Beechmast nuts – Found beneath beech trees, these brown kernels are identified by their arrow-shaped shells and are a great alternative to chestnuts for snacking without cooking. To eat them you need to peel off the shell by cracking it open and simply eat the flesh inside. Due to their high fat content, years ago the oil from these was used for cooking.

Common sorrel – This oval-shaped green leaf can be recognised by the two lobes at the base which point downwards. It grows on grassy banks and low down on hillsides. Slightly sour to taste, it's great in salads and can be added to sandwiches or cooked like spinach.

Common Sorrel

Nettles – Most of us are already familiar with these stinging plants, which are found in moist woodlands and along rivers and mainly regarded as a nuisance. But once infused they can make a tasty beverage. Only use the younger, smaller ones and wear gardening gloves to avoid being stung, then, after washing them, simply boil until the water goes green. Remove the leaves and add some lemon or sugar for flavour. Tea's up!

Wild garlic – Often found in ancient woodland, this can be identified by its clusters of white flowers and long, spear-shaped leaves. You'll be struck by a strong garlicky aroma when you've found them. You can chop up the leaves and flowers and add them to salads and soup or sauces, or for something a bit special, brush bread with olive oil and toast, then finely chop and sprinkle leaves on the top.

TOP UP YOUR FIRST AID KIT

Forget something? Never mind, you might just find it's been provided for by Mother Nature herself...

Sphagnum moss: A favourite of bushcrafters such as Ray Mears, this green, peaty moss has antiseptic properties. So if you scratch yourself or get a small cut when camping, this is perfect to clean the wound – you simply rub the leaves (which will be watery) over the affected area. AND, it's also great for cleaning out your bowls and cups if you have no washing-up liquid! It's soft to the touch, and can be recognised by its tiny leaves which can be toothed, grow in tufts close to the stem and are usually light green.

Find it: On boggy ground in large patches.

Birch polypore fungi: Got carried away walking and now have a sore on your foot? Help is at hand! Large, white, shaped like shelves and always growing horizontally on trees, this spongy, non-toxic (though non-edible) specimen contains antibiotics. It is very absorbent and naturally cooling, anti-inflammatory and anti-bacterial – perfect for soothing blisters. It's also easy to cut into any shape. It was found on the mummified body of Ötzi the Iceman in the Alps, who even back in 3300 BC had cottoned onto its medical benefits.

Find it: Growing on decaying trees in dark places in forests.

Foxglove leaves: Forgot the loo roll? Happens to us all. If you're caught short and really can't wait, look out for these large, soft green leaves (usually oval in shape and quite wide, with soft, short hairs on the upper surface) found on the stems of purple bell-shaped foxglove flowers – they make for great emergency velvety toilet paper.

Find it: Near rivers in areas of high foliage.

Wood sorrel: Though perhaps not strictly first aid for a medical emergency, this tangy clover-shaped leaf – identified by the absence of the pale V-shape on each leaf that is found on true clover – is a great toothpaste substitute.

Find it: In woodlands near to lakes.

SOURCE WATER

When camping, you should always seek your H_2O from a fast-flowing stream or tarn and purify it by boiling it, using a filter or adding purification tablets. However, if you do find yourself out in the wild in a place where water is clearly prevalent and saturating the ground but not on the surface, you can – in an emergency – dig a well. Simply:

1. Dig a hole about 15 centimetres across, near to a muddy pond or similar.

2. Keep going until the hole starts filling with water.

3. Remove the first and second lots of water, then after the third time collect it into a container.

4. Filter and boil it to sterilise it before drinking.

5. If you will need more water from it later, cover your hole with a stone so that no wildlife gets in it.

MAKE SOMETHING USEFUL

Reeds are a great weapon in the bushcrafter's arsenal. Found by rivers and streams, they are strong yet easy to bend and twist, they can be shaped to make containers, mend snapped cord and even fashioned into cutlery. But for something very simple, why not try to make your own mat?

1. Cut reeds long enough to horizontally fit under your bottom.

2. Gather together a clump that when held in your hand is approximately 5–6 centimetres in diameter and lash together with string on both ends. Don't cut the ends of the string as you'll want to use it to add more clumps.

3. Get another clump of reeds, the same length and diameter as the first one, and use the ends of the string to secure these to the last clump.

4. Repeat until you have enough sections – probably about ten.

5. Secure the ends of the string tightly and cut off any excess reed.

READING THE SIGNS

The more you know, the less you carry.

MORS KOCHANSKI

P redicting the weather, navigating by the stars – there's so much scope for understanding our natural world without modern technology and a camping trip is the perfect opportunity to try it... Plus, you'll have a slew of nifty tricks to impress your friends!

Predict the Weather

Weather can change quickly, especially if you're up in mountain country; even if you're lower down, watching what happens higher up can help you see what's coming to you later. Checking the forecast before you head out on a camping trip is obviously ideal, but there are some warning signs to watch for in the sky:

Cirrus clouds – Look for streams of cloud that can be seen to move and curl over ridges as these warn that conditions could deteriorate.

Cumulonimbus towers – Huge heaps of vertical clouds accumulating in the distance with a flat top can be a sign of thunder or heavy rain on its way.

Halo around the moon – This is caused by the light coming through a sheet-like cirrostratus cloud and is a sign of snow or rain coming.

USE THE NORTH STAR

You can find the North Star using the saucepan-shaped Plough constellation.

1. Pick out the two stars that form the edge of the 'pan' furthest from the 'handle'.

2. Hold up your arm and line up those stars against the edge of your hand.

3. Follow this angle for four times the distance between these stars.

4. This will take you to the North Star – a very bright star. Once facing this you know you're roughly facing north, with west to your left and east to your right.

Night Navigation

To work out which way you're facing you need use only the stars:

1. Select a star in the sky and push a stick into the ground (or place a stone) vertically underneath where it is to mark its position.

2. Wait for 30 minutes and go back to where you left your marker. Because the earth rotates your star will no longer be above your marker. Look at where it now is in relation to the marker.

3. If the star is now...
   ... left, you're looking north.
   ... right, you're looking south.
   ... down, you're looking west.
   ... up, you're looking east.

To help you remember: 'Lost Nomads Die Wondering', which is 'Left North, Down West'; from that you can work out the other directions. It's worth noting that this applies in the northern hemisphere; you'll have to adjust the directions accordingly in the southern.

NAVIGATE WITH NATURE

When walking you should always take a map and compass, but there are several ways you can start to learn natural navigation – you just need to know where to look...

Trees – The side that faces the sun will have bark that is noticeably thinner – this will be south if you're in the northern hemisphere. As a general rule, trees also bend away from the prevailing wind (roughly south-west), and more branches grow on the sheltered side (north-east).

Shadows – Take a branch and stick it in the ground. Put a stone at the end of the shadow it casts. Wait half an hour and mark the end of the new shadow with another stone. The line that runs between these two should run approximately east–west.

Vegetation – Normally flowers tend to face south as that's where they get the most sun, so have a look and see which way they're pointed.

FIND SOUTH WITH YOUR WATCH

This is simple but requires a watch with a face – it will not work on a digital one!

1. Line up the hour hand with the sun.

2. Imagine a line that cuts through the watch face at the midway point between the 12 and the hour hand.

3. This line will indicate which way is south.

A TRICK TO IMPRESS YOUR FRIENDS

Deer are still quite prevalent in the British landscape and spotting their tracks when walking in woodlands or open countryside and even in campsites themselves is very common. But what if you could actually tell whether a female or male deer had been walking there? It might not help you cook the night's dinner but it could impress your partner/kids/friends enough to persuade them to do the washing-up!

All deer tracks will create a foot-on-foot pattern as they place their hind legs in the same spot where their front legs have been. The females have a wider gait between their back legs as they have wider hips to aid giving birth. The males have a wider gait between their front legs, as they are broader for strength. So when you look at the tracks you need to simply work out whether or not the back legs or the front legs are wider apart.

Female tracks – The second set of prints that overlay the first ones should overlap on the outside edges.

Male tracks – The second overlaying prints should fall inside the first set of prints.

GLAMPING

Is that weird, taking my Louis
Vuitton bag camping?

JESSICA SIMPSON

GLAMPING

It had to happen eventually. Once Kate Moss was seen traipsing through a field in tight trendy denim shorts and Hunter wellies at a festival in 2007, boasting of her ability to 'rough it' in a luxury tent behind the scenes, then faster than Gok Wan could say 'it's all about the confidence', camping got a makeover.

No longer was it about going back to nature, getting your fingernails dirty, shunning the shower and digging your own latrine. No, now it was about who made your tent, how much you could get your overnight accommodation to feel like the interior of an upmarket London studio and how many electric items you could operate from your generator – a kind of caravan under canvas, designed to make the outdoors as comfortable as the indoors and twice as cool.

Suddenly Ted Baker, Zandra Rhodes, Laura Ashley and Cath Kidston were on the scene, designing tents for fashionistas that were made to make your fellow campers green with envy. Manufacturers jumped on the bandwagon with portable sit-down toilets, lightweight wine coolers, gas-canister-operated tent heaters, sleeping bags you could wear, mini French presses for fresh coffee in your tent and camping stoves bigger and better than most indoor cookers.

Glamping – a happy medium between glamour and camping – is easily found in one of the new glampsites that have sprung up. Staples include yurts with real oak flooring and electric lighting and shabby chic tepees complete with designer sheets for the real bed – no sleeping mat required! Glampers do love the outdoors, but they also love their creature comforts and don't see any reason why the two have to be mutually exclusive. So for a night of upmarket outdoor living – for a slightly inflated price tag (expect to pay £100 per night upwards for proper luxury) – why not forget the hassle of pitching your own tent and opt for a sumptuous canvas lodge? You never know, darling – after sampling its delights you might never be able to head out for a night of camping without your caviar again…

For glamping options check out http://goglamping.net.

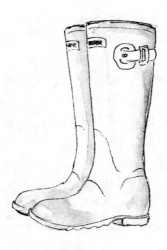

YOUR KNOW YOU'RE A GLAMPER WHEN...

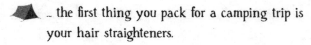

... the first thing you pack for a camping trip is your hair straighteners.

... your campsite neighbours are Pete Doherty and Lily Allen.

... lights out involves using an actual light switch.

... your walking boots are made by UGG.

... other campers come by to borrow a cup of Chateau Lafayette.

... you see the printed phrase 'do not get wet' anywhere on your kit.

... you look down on your neighbours because their tent is 'so last season'.

THE ULTIMATE GLAMPERS' TENT – THE YURT

Still used in Mongolia and the Middle East as mobile homes, these structures offer glampers maximum comfort for minimum effort. Essentially a yurt is a portable, lattice wooden-framed structure with thick walls made of felt to keep the heat in (traditionally made from wool from the owner's sheep herd). Nowadays the yurts that glampers go for are heated by solid-fuel-burning stoves and in a lot of cases feature electric lights and even fridges! Though the real yurts are designed to be easily dismantled and carried to a new location courtesy of camels, the glamorous variety are usually much more permanent and are rented rather than owned by campers.

DON'T JUST SLEEP IN IT – WEAR IT!

It may sound crazy but ask any hardened fashionista and they will tell you that tents have even made it onto the catwalk. In 2004 Adrienne Pao and Robin Lasser both designed tents that you wear – from street-wear camo numbers to yurt-inspired wedding gowns.

CONTROVERSIAL CANVAS

You know that camping has gone glam when even the art world starts to look to it for inspiration. And in 1995 the often provocative British artist Tracey Emin made a tent the talking point of the world. Entitled *Everyone I Have Ever Slept With 1963–1995*, but often referred to as 'The Tent', it featured a standard-looking dome structure that had the names of 102 people stitched to the walls inside. A lot of people assumed it referred to people she'd had sex with, though it actually just meant those she'd shared a bed with, e.g. her grandma, and thus it became one of her most debated and divisive works of art. This iconic piece was bought by serial Brit Art collector Charles Saatchi, but was destroyed in 2004 when the Momart warehouse caught fire. Despite several offers Emin has refused to remake it.

DID YOU KNOW?

Even in death some still like to take glamping to a new level. Nineteenth-century explorer Sir Richard Burton's mausoleum in Mortlake, Surrey, is in the form of an Eastern traveller's tent, tall enough for him to have stood up in, with strings of camel bells hanging from the ceiling.

TENT-ER-TAINMENT

*Happiness flutters in the air whilst we
rest among the breaths of nature.*

KELLY SCHEAFFER

T ent-bound due to bad weather? Find yourself at a loose end without a TV, Facebook and games consoles to keep you busy? Feel like being sociable? Especially if you've got kids to entertain, here are some tent-ative ideas...

HOW TO PASS TIME IN A TENT
(AND HAVE FUN TOO)

Spot stars – It's always fun to gaze at the sky and name some of the obvious constellations – Plough, anyone? If you don't know any, why not try to find your own shapes by dot-to-dotting the tiny twinkles?

Tell stories – Take it in turns to be the storyteller, making up a tale using camping items around you, e.g. your head torch, water bottles. Once it gets dark scary stories are always best and you can use a torch for dramatic effect. Cue horror movie laugh – mwah ha ha hah hah!

Make some music – It's no surprise that the guitar is a classic campsite instrument because all you need is a few chords and a popular song to get people singing along. So take some time to learn a few ditties – before long you'll get everyone joining in. Everybody: 'Kum-ba-yah...'

Do shadow puppets – Always a favourite with young and old alike. Make it into a story as you go. Extra points to anyone who can do more than a standard rabbit!

Exercise – Chances are you'll be cold at some point, especially when the sun goes down, so get up, move around, stretch, even jog on the spot or dance. Fun and good for you.

Talk – Maybe an obvious idea but now really is the perfect time to get to know each other better and utilise this time to bond.

Do nothing – It really is OK just to lie back and relax you know – try it and you'll see that this can be the best way to pass time in a tent of all.

A Funny Campsite Fireside Story...

The fire was dying down by their campsite as Sherlock Holmes addressed Dr Watson. Holmes, lying on his blanket, asked: 'Watson, tell me what you see up there.'

'Ah, a wondrous array of brilliant stars,' replied Watson.

'And what, dear Watson, does that tell you?' asked Holmes.

Watson replied: 'It is testament to billions of other galaxies with similar densities of stars, possibly trillions of planets associated with them. With such numbers and a similar chemical distribution in all the cosmos, a man might infer the likelihood of intelligent life up there.

'What's more, theologically, the great vastness of that wondrous space indicates the greatness of God, a reminder that we are mere mortals of minor significance.

'If we consider the sky meteorologically, its blackness and the clear brilliance of the stars suggests decreased humidity and stable air, which could well lead to a clear day on the morrow.'

'Would you add more, Mr Watson? How would you conclude?' asked Holmes.

'Well,' replied Watson philosophically, 'looking up there, I'd say that somebody has stolen our tent.'

WEATHERBOUND?

Rain can be a pain when camping but just because you can't get out and explore, it doesn't mean you have to do nothing. Why not try...

Play – Taking a deck of cards is always a good idea just in case; if not, there's always I spy...

Tidy – Making your new home organised can be a really satisfying thing to do, as well as being practical.

Socialise – Offering cups of tea to neighbours is a great way to get to know each other; you may well have a lot in common and before you know it, the sun will be out again.

Write – Embrace one of very few moments of quiet contemplation in our otherwise hectic world to scribble down your thoughts, whether in a journal or on a postcard to a friend; it's therapeutic and gets your creativity flowing.

SOME MURPHY'S LAWS OF CAMPING

1. The urge to go to the toilet once it's dark will intensify in exact relation to the amount of people you'll have to disturb, the amount of rain that has fallen and the number of bags you'll need to rummage through to find your head torch.

2. It is a known fact that once free of any walking shoes your feet with expand. The same rule applies to sleeping bags when removed from their compression sacks, and contents from your rucksack.

3. Even if there's as little as a 10 per cent chance of rain, you can be certain that 99 per cent of it will fall on your tent.

IN TENTS READING

For those slow afternoons, why not try losing yourself in:

Walden; Or, Life in the Woods by Henry D. Thoreau
The story of one man's social experiment to become self-sufficient by building himself a shelter in the woods where he lived for two years in 1845–47.

A Walk in the Woods by Bill Bryson
This hilariously witty book sees Bill taking us on his journey of an attempt to walk the world's longest long-distance path in America with his trusty tent and a healthy fear of bears.

Lost in the Jungle by Yossi Ghinsberg
A true tale of survival from the man who went into the Amazon jungle for adventure and emerged unscathed... just!

CAMPFIRE CLASSICS

Easy to play on a guitar... and guaranteed to get fellow campers singing along:

'Jessie's Girl' – Rick Springfield
'The Passenger' – Iggy Pop
'Redemption Song' – Bob Marley
'House of the Rising Sun' – The Animals
'Hey Jude' – The Beatles

BEING GREEN

Take only photographs, leave only footprints.

NATURALIST PROVERB

Feeling green? Pat yourself on the back. By being a camper you're already partaking in one of the greenest activities there is. Of all the different ways of holidaying, the actual act of spending the night under a temporary structure like a tent leaves a tiny carbon footprint – especially if you do it in the UK. But there are always ways of being even friendlier to the environment...

THE CAMPER'S GUIDE TO BEING GREENER

Ditch the car – By getting to your campsite via public transport or better yet by cycling or walking, you'll not only save some money but also help save the planet.

Conserve water – If you've got some left in your stove from cooking a boil-in-the-bag meal, use it to wash your pots, or let it cool and use it to brush your teeth.

Save fuel – If you are camping in a group don't all cook separately: if you can cook two meals together you'll make your fuel go further and there will be no food envy, as you will eat at the same time.

Look after your gear – Every year, kit ends up in landfill because people haven't taken the time to look after it so it stops working properly. For tips on repairing and caring for your tent, see Camping SOS chapter.

Invest in alternative energy – From iPod and mobile phone chargers powered by the sun to wind-up torches and radios, you don't always need to rely on batteries.

Recycle – You may be away from home, but that doesn't mean you have to stop recycling. Divide up your rubbish so that you can dispose of everything properly either at the campsite or when you get home.

*Nature halts self-absorption,
makes you less frantic about all
that's going on in your own
small mental or physical world.*

MARGARET DRABBLE

CAMPSITES DOING THEIR BIT

You'll often find that because campers love the outdoors, many campsite owners do all they can to be as eco-friendly as possible. Before choosing your next site why not see if it does any of the following:

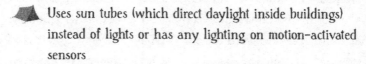

- Uses sun tubes (which direct daylight inside buildings) instead of lights or has any lighting on motion-activated sensors

- Uses solar or wind-powered energy in buildings/facilities

- Reuses rainwater for flushing toilets

- Takes part in a tree-planting programme

- Discourages the use of vehicles on site

How Can I Be Sure?

There are various awards and accolades that campsites can pick up when they've proved their green commitment. One of these is the David Bellamy Conservation Award – which can be awarded in gold, silver and bronze levels. Accreditation is gained after local environmental experts and Conservation Foundation assessors have evaluated the site. Sir David Bellamy, the hugely respected environmentalist and the scheme's namesake, has even had a say in the independent assessment that is also undertaken. They are marked on key elements such as: energy efficiency, green energy purchase, light pollution, resourcing local materials, reduction of waste and water conservation.

TOP FIVE ECO-FRIENDLY CAMPSITES

1. **The Quiet Site, Lake District, Cumbria**

   www.thequietsite.co.uk

   Holder of the David Bellamy Gold Award, this site harvests flush water, uses low-energy lighting, recycles, heats water with solar power, sources materials and food locally and uses biodegradable products for cleaning.

2. **Eco Retreats, Dyfi Valley, Powys**

   www.ecoretreats.co.uk

   You might not be able to take your tent but once you're nestled in one of the tepees in this 1,300-acre organic farm you won't care. While here, check out the Centre for Alternative Technology in Machynlleth for some eco-tips!

3. **South Penquite, Bodmin Moor, Cornwall**

   www.southpenquite.co.uk

   Stay on an organic farm and enjoy feeling smugly carbon free as you indulge in a solar-heated rainwater shower where the walls are lined with recycled bottles and you still get to enjoy the views from Bodmin Moor.

4. **The Dome Garden, Forest of Dean, Gloucestershire**

www.domegarden.co.uk

OK, so you'll have to use one of their geodesic domes, but you will definitely be doing your bit because the watchword here is ecosystems. You heat your own water as you heat the dome, using logs from the local forest in a wood-burning stove, and the excess heat is driven down into the insulated boxes of recycled glass under the floor by a solar fan and can be used in the night when it has gotten cold – genius!

5. **Camusdarach, West Highlands, Scotland**

www.camusdarach.com

Not only does this site boast a stunning seaside location but the owners have done all they can to make everything sustainable, including a shower block that has been designed to make the outflow water become detoxified by surrounding plants.

Camping SOS

It always rains on tents. Rainstorms will travel thousands of miles, against prevailing winds, for the opportunity to rain on a tent.

Dave Barry

A worn-out tent is the sign of a proper camper, adventures had and memorable nights, but to get more life out of your tent – and keep it out the landfill – you just need to take care of it. Better yet, it only takes a few minutes.

DRYING YOUR TENT

One of the worst mistakes you can make as a camper is to wake up following heavy rain and cram your tent back into its stuff sack. You're bound to leave it there when you get home then, next time you come to use it, wonder why it has a musty smell and damp patches. Whether it's dew, condensation or rain, you want to get it off your tent before you pack it away. Here's what to do:

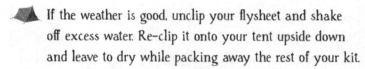 If the weather is good, unclip your flysheet and shake off excess water. Re-clip it onto your tent upside down and leave to dry while packing away the rest of your kit.

Before you roll away the inner or (if applicable) separate groundsheet, wipe off as much water as you can using a towel or chamois.

Once home: even if you managed to do the above before you left your campsite, unpack your tent and shake it off again. If there is still water on it, hang it to dry either on your washing line or over your bathtub. Only pack it away once it's completely dry.

Remember to clean and dry your tent pegs to stop them getting rusty.

WET, WET, WET

Though most of the time people mistake condensation for a leaking tent, it is important to keep an eye on it in case over the years the fabric loses its waterproofness. The first thing you need to do is establish whether or not it's really leaking. The best way to do this is to erect it in your garden on a rainy day and check to see if water is coming in. With no one inside creating condensation, the results will tell you what the problem is:

Lost waterproofness – This can happen over time. If you've not dried or cleaned your tent properly after a bad weather trip that can be the root cause, so try wiping off all the mud and debris first (do not ever use detergent as this can ruin the proofer). Once it's clean you can apply a reproofer such as Nikwax or Grangers; these should do the trick. They are usually sprayed on or rubbed over the fabric – read the instructions carefully before use.

Leaking seams – If the water is only coming in through the places where the fabric is sewn together, then the seam sealer must have worn away. You can buy a tube of sealer very inexpensively from most outdoor stores and tent manufacturers. Apply to the tent only when it's dry and give it plenty of time to dry – usually a day or two.

DID YOU KNOW?

Duct tape is a fantastic fix-all accessory to take with you on camping trips. From ripped groundsheets to leaking seams, it can temporarily repair a multitude of problems. Well worth taking in the car or, if wild camping, wrap some around one of your walking poles so it stays sticky.

Keep Sleeping Soundly...

It's not just your tent that needs looking after; your sleeping bag and mat also need storing and cleaning properly to keep them useful for as long as possible.

Storing your sleeping bag – Never store your sleeping bag in your stuff sack as this will compress the down inside it, which reduces its insulating capabilities. You need to store it in a bigger bag – a bin bag can do – so that the feathers can move around. Put it somewhere it won't get damp.

Storing your sleeping mats – Mats should be stored with the valves left open, unfolded under a settee or bed.

Washing your sleeping bag – Always read the instructions on your particular model first but as a general rule...

... if it's synthetic, machine wash with pure soap flakes on a gentle cycle. Once finished place in the dryer on a cool setting with tennis balls inside to separate any clumps of damp insulation.

... if it's down, hand-wash in your bath using warm water and either pure soap or a specialist cleaning product (Grangers/Nikwax). Submerge your bag and move it around, squeezing gently. Leave for half an hour then move around again and squeeze. Empty the bath then roll the sleeping bag carefully to squeeze out excess water. Rinse by filling the bath again with warm water and squeeze bag as before. Repeat several times, until the soap disappears. If it fits in your washing machine, put it on a gentle spin, otherwise let it drip dry. Keep it somewhere warm and airy for several days to absorb the remaining moisture, shaking occasionally to loosen clumps. Don't bag it until the down is free-moving, fluffy and completely dry.

Beat the Bugs

Mosquitos remind us that we're not as high up the food chain as we think.

Tom Wilson

There are so many great things you can experience when sleeping and living under canvas but as with everything, it's not perfect – there can be some annoying pests that you have to deal with from time to time. But don't fret, there's always a way to beat the bugs...

Ticks

What they are
Tiny parasites that are part of the spider family.

Where you'll find them
All over the UK in sheep- or deer-grazed grass and woodland – so they can be a real problem when wild camping.

What they look like
At first glance a tiny black dot – which is why it's often hard to know that you have one on you. But under a microscope they are eight-legged bugs with tiny heads and larger bodies, which swell as they feed.

Why they're a problem
They burrow their heads down into your skin to feed on your blood, but you won't feel them doing it because as well as being tiny they also inject you with an anaesthetic when they bite. The bite itself won't cause a problem but ticks can be carriers of the bacteria that causes Lyme disease – easily treatable with antibiotics if detected early on, but can be difficult to diagnose.

Tick

How to deal with them

Don't panic. Using a pair of straight-tipped tweezers grip the creature as close to its jaws as possible and pull it straight out (without twisting or turning it) – the trick is to get every part of it out in one. Various implements are available to buy to remove them safely but if you're unsure seek medical help.

MIDGES

What they are

Essentially tiny biting flies, there are over forty different known species of midge in Scotland alone. They detect you by body odour and the carbon dioxide you breathe out.

Where they are

Anywhere in Britain, but a real problem in Scotland during May–September, especially near standing water and in woodland and even on high mountains. They're more prevalent at dusk and dawn.

What they look like

Small flies, but the sting you feel as they bite you gives them away.

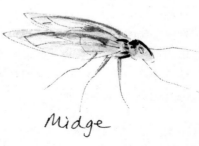

Midge

Why they're a problem
They can be relentless and travel in swarms so you never get just one bite, but several, and they itch and sting for days afterwards – not severely but enough to be a nuisance.

How to deal with them
The one thing they can't deal with is wind, so even a gentle breeze will keep them away. They also tend to be attracted to dark colours so you can try adjusting your wardrobe. Repellents can be used (see below) as can special midge hats with netting to protect your face, but they key is to avoid them in the first place. Check online at www.midgeforecast.co.uk where nuisance levels of the little blighters are rated geographically.

HORSEFLIES

What they are
Also called clegs, they are large flies (some up to 2 centimetres in length).

Where they are
In fields and hedgerows, usually close to water on sunny, still days in the summertime.

Horsefly

What they look like
A bit like wasps but often bigger.

Why they're a problem
Their bite can be very painful as they slice through your skin and cause a sore rash in some people.

How to deal with them
Repellents are key to keeping these away.

WASPS

What they are
Stinging flying insects.

Where they are
Seemingly everywhere in the outdoors during the summer – normally when you're trying to enjoy your barbeque or picnic.

Wasp

What they look like
Yellow and black with a thinner body than bees.

Why they're a problem

Usually, as long as you don't flap around when they come near you, they won't be a problem; however, come the end of the summer when they begin to die off they can get aggravated and sting without any reason, which is very painful and can cause an allergic reaction in some people.

How to deal with them

If you keep still and don't panic, they should leave you alone, but if you do get stung some people swear by using vinegar as the acid in it can neutralise the alkaline in the sting.

REPELLENTS

Insect repellents are a good way to keep the bugs at bay, and the experts recommend using those that contain DEET. However, this is not necessarily recommended for small children and some people would prefer to avoid it. A good DEET-free alternative is citronella oil (though this will need frequent reapplication) and in Scotland, to keep midges off, Avon Skin So Soft is highly recommended.

POST-STING/BITE

Whether you've been unlucky with bugs or caught out by a stinging nettle, you'll want to keep some form of after-bite in your camping first-aid kit. Wash and dry the area first then try either chamomile lotion or cream containing hydrocortisone such as Anthisan.

CAMPER'S FRIENDS

Though not everyone's cup of tea, we campers really should learn to love...

Spiders – These eight-legged arachnids won't hurt you and will actually help to keep numbers of midges and the like down by feeding on them.

Bats – Coming out at dusk, these flying creatures can gobble up lots of the flies that pester us.

EXTREME SLEEPS

We're not home-and-hearth people. We're the adventurers, the buccaneers, the blockade runners. Without challenge, we're only alive.

ALEXANDRA RIPLEY

Though anyone who's spent the night in a windy tent in a rainstorm can quite rightly claim they've roughed it, there are some people who would think that was child's play. There are definitely those who, when it comes to lights out, truly push the ZZZZs to the max!

CRAZY CLIMBERS

When pitching a tent we know that it's important to check the ground first for uncomfortable rocks or sinking bogs – but what if there's no ground there at all? This is a common issue for big wall climbers who take on week-long adventures – every day of them on a vertical cliff face! As they can't simply pop down to the campsite after each day's section of a climb when tackling mammoth routes like Half Dome in Yosemite, California, they need something that allows them to sleep safely. Enter portaledging.

Though climbers have traditionally bivvyed on precarious rocky ledges, for sheer faces where there are no natural ledges to perch on the portaledge is a fantastic invention. Like tepees on steroids these triangular single-skin structures are secured to rock faces using ropes and karabiners and literally suspended above hundreds of metres of nothingness so that the inhabitant can (supposedly) settle down to a restful night's sleep.

You do have some security in that you sleep with a climbing harness on and are secured to the rock independently from your shelter but still, you have to ask just how reassuring that would be in a high wind...

THERE'S SNOW PLACE LIKE HOLE

Come the winter the vast majority of campers will pack away the tent pegs until the warmer days of spring. But there are a select bunch who will carry on regardless, some winter camping and others taking it one step further – with a snow hole.

Literally a hole dug into snow, these are actually meant for use during life and death scenarios, and you can go on courses to learn this survival technique. It's not recommended that you do it without expert training but roughly it involves deep snow (of the right consistency), a steep slope and a shovel. Here are the basics:

1. You need to dig an entrance, big enough for you to crawl in, directly into the snow slope.

2. Dig upwards to construct your main chamber, keeping walls at least a foot in thickness. It is vital that you dig up, not down, to stop wind blowing in.

3. Continue digging, pushing snow back out through the entrance, until it's big enough for you to lie down and sit or stand comfortably.

4. Create a ventilation hole using an ice axe or shovel handle.

DID YOU KNOW?

The highest base camp in the world is on Mount Everest, located at 5,545 metres above sea level on the northern (Tibetan) side of the world's highest mountain. The one that most trekkers visit on guided tours is on the southern (Nepalese) side, but is lower at 5,364 metres. Still, ask anyone who's been and they'll tell you it's no easier to get to!

MILLICAN DALTON (1867–1947)

How did an insurance clerk from Essex become the cave man of Borrowdale? Millican Dalton was living a pretty conventional life but at the age of thirty-six found office work too dull to bear. He sold his terrace house for an acre of land where he lived in a tent then decided to take the next step, leaving London and heading north for a new life in the Lake District. In the early 1900s he established himself as a 'Professor of Adventure' and carved out a living as a mountain guide offering visitors experiences such as camping, rock-climbing, ghyll-scrambling (scaling narrow mountain streams) and rafting.

A great believer in self-reliance, when he wasn't guiding he used the knowledge he had gained working in the outdoors to design new and innovative lightweight equipment – thought to be some of the earliest forms of its kind.

Perhaps one of the most extreme sleepers, once he left the city he spent the rest of his life sleeping and living outside – under canvas, in makeshift bivvies, in a hut and, most famously, during the summer, in a cave which he dubbed 'The Cave Hotel' in the Lakes. Nestled on the eastern flanks of Castle Crag, the spacious, split-level apartment (consisting of connecting caves) had a constant supply of water that ran through a crack in the ceiling.

He quickly became something of a celebrity in nearby Keswick, instantly recognisable due to his home-made clothes. Clearly a man ahead of his time – a pacifist, vegetarian and teetotaller who grew his own food – he thought nothing of hosting mixed-sex camping parties, which were completely taboo at the time, and helped a great many women learn to climb when other guides wouldn't have taken them out.

At the age of 79, during the winter the hut he stayed in down south to escape the colder temperatures burned down, and he moved into a tent instead. Sadly, this proved too much for him and he died of pneumonia shortly after in Amersham Hospital.

He called his cave in Borrowdale home for the best part of fifty years and, until recently when a partial collapse made it unsafe, people would go and pay it a visit. Inside he left some words of wisdom carved into the rock of the upper chamber. It quite simply states: 'Don't waste words, jump to conclusions.'

STRANGE BUT TRUE

In 2011 Yorkshireman Andy Strangeway set himself the challenge of doing the six most extreme sleeps in Britain – and succeeded. He slept at the highest and lowest points of the country (Ben Nevis in Scotland and Holme Fen in Cambridgeshire) as well as the northern, southern, western and easternmost reaches of the UK. But he was already no stranger to waking up in odd places; in 2007 he slept on all of Scotland's 162 islands.

Child's Play

Nature teaches more than she preaches.
There are no sermons in stones.

John Burroughs

There's no better way to reinvigorate your love for camping than by introducing the activity to your kids. Not only will it take them away from TVs, mobile phones and games consoles, it will also expose them to the many joys of the outdoors while allowing you to spend quality time with them.

KEEP THEM INTERESTED

Here are some easy ways to make sure your children enjoy their camping experience:

Get them involved – Though it might be easier (and probably quicker) to pitch the tent and sort out the bedding yourself, this is the perfect time to make them feel part of it and enjoy the pride felt when the tent's up. So whether it's hammering in pegs or blowing up mattresses, let them do it.

Bring backup – Though nature provides lots of things they can do – e.g. watch stars, paddle in streams or climb trees – it's always best to have some games ready to crack open to keep them busy and avoid the dreaded cries of 'I'm bored'. Take a frisbee, football, kite, cricket bat and more for great easy activities you can all play together.

Let them cook – From toasting marshmallows over a campfire (if permitted) to enlisting their help preparing kebabs, letting them cook will not only help them feel useful but also teach them to be self-sufficient.

Comfort is key – Children will feel the cold so make sure you bring plenty of warm layers for them, squishy pillows and even a proper duvet to make the tent seem like home. A well-rested kid is a happy kid!

DID YOU KNOW?

In 2010 The Camping and Caravanning Club asked 1,000 adults who camped regularly, and 1,000 who had never camped before, how they felt on an average day. The campers were generally more satisfied, happy, optimistic and energised, whereas the non-campers were more stressed, frustrated, bored and lonely.

KIDDIES KIT

If you're taking your children camping, it's great to give them their own rucksack to make them feel grown-up. But what should you pack for them?

Torch – For night-time. Great for creating shadow puppets.

Water bottle – A small one will be fine and there are lots of bright-coloured options.

Snacks – Take some treats to keep them motivated.

Favourite toy – In case everything else fails to impress.

TOP TEN CHILD-FRIENDLY CAMPSITES

1. **Side Farm, Lake District, Cumbria**
    01768 482337
    Set on the shores of Ullswater amid fantastic fell-side scenery,
    this campsite scores extra points for keeping the kids happy
    as from here you can also board one of the old steam-powered
    boats to Glenridding and enjoy a great stroll back.

2. **Gordale Scar Campsite, Skipton, North Yorkshire**
    01729 830333
    There might not be rides or farm animals to keep the kids
    entertained, but there is the scenery of Malham Cove nearby,
    made famous in the blockbusting film *Harry Potter and the
    Deathly Hallows (Part 1)*. Harry and Hermione camped on
    top of this stunning limestone cliff, and for the kids, waking
    up below it will be just as exciting.

3. **Featherdown Farm, locations nationwide**
    01420 80804; www.featherdown.co.uk
    This place takes camping to the next level, offering tented
    accommodation that includes running water and proper beds.
    It's a great place to get your little 'uns interested in the idea
    of sleeping outdoors and the fact that it's a farm means they
    get to learn about the animals and join in with activities like
    collecting eggs, too.

4. **Greenacres, Shepton Mallet, Somerset**
   01749 890497; www.greenacres-camping.co.uk
   A proper, old-fashioned, family-friendly campsite, this one offers a range of apparatus to keep the kids happy, from a proper football pitch to toys, see-saws, swings, Wendy houses, bikes to hire and books to read; the kids will be kept busy so you can relax.

5. **Eweleaze Farm, Osmington, Dorset**
   01305 833690; www.eweleaze.co.uk
   Boasting a private section of beach which you can access straight from the site, it's no wonder that this place is a hit with families. Add to that a farm shop and the best views in the area and this is a hard one to beat!

6. **Dan yr Ogof, Brecon Beacons**
   01639 730284; www.showcaves.co.uk
   An animal farm, a dinosaur park, limestone caves and quirky rock formations all on the doorstep; head to this site safe in the knowledge that the little tykes will definitely be kept busy.

7. **Snowdonia Park Campsite, Snowdonia National Park, Gwynedd**

   01286 650409; www.snowdonia-park.co.uk

   Steam trains are a fantastic way to capture young imaginations and this place makes it even easier as the site itself is actually a stop on the Welsh Highland Railway. From here you can explore Caernarfon Castle or let the train take the strain as you head into the national park's fantastic mountain scenery.

8. **Pencarnan Farm, St David's, Pembrokeshire**

   01437 720580; www.pembrokeshirecamping.co.uk

   Just 3 miles away from the hustle and bustle of seaside town St David's you can relax on this site's private beach and spend hours exploring rock pools with your kids – bliss!

9. **Beecraigs Country Park, Linlithgow, West Lothian**
   01506 844516; www.beecraigs.com
   There's so much going on that it will be difficult to decide what not to do with your children while here. Choose from watching the majestic stags at the deer farm, visiting the rainbow trout at the fishery, trying a forest trail, rowing a boat or going to the activity centre for archery or an attempt at the climbing wall – phew, feeling tired yet?

10. **Sands Country Park, Gairloch, Wester Ross**
    01445 712152; www.sandsholidaycentre.co.uk
    Pitch up between the sand dunes then get set for some serious water sports – windsurfing, kayaking or a dinghy ride. Certain to entertain teens as well as younger kids.

FESTIVAL CAMPING

*We all love Glastonbury. It gives us the
chance to put our Gucci wellies on!*

NICOLE APPLETON

For many people a festival can be their first foray into the world of camping for pleasure. It can ignite a love affair with the outdoors – the realisation that you don't need much to be comfortable, the camaraderie, and the sense of pride that comes with building your own shelter. But, if done wrong, what with the sheer volume of people and the extra vigilance needed to avoid crime, you can be put off outdoor living for life. But with a bit of planning, some useful know-how and a few simple adaptations to usual camping habits, it can be one of the most memorable times you'll have.

Festival Dos and Don'ts

Do make sure you can carry all your camping gear from your car in a bag – you won't get to park alongside your pitch here.

Do get there early; this can make a difference between getting a prime spot and one on boggy ground, downwind of the toilets.

Do lower your expectations of facilities offered. The toilets may well look adequate on day one, but by day three...

Do make your tent recognisable. There will be other green dome tents there besides yours, so tie on some ribbons, mark it with your name or pitch near a landmark to help you relocate it – especially after a few drinks!

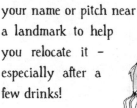

Do take earplugs – a field full of snorers can be hard to sleep through.

Don't take your most expensive camping gear – it might get ruined or, worst-case scenario, stolen.

Don't camp too near the toilets, the fast-food kiosks or the bins – it might be convenient but you will regret it.

Don't forget your head torch – once night falls all the tents will disappear into the darkness and you don't want to spend the evening apologising as you fall over everyone else's guy lines.

Don't leave valuables in your tent, keep them with you at all times.

Don't keep your tent tidy; though it's great to be organised, a festival is not the place to do it. If you leave things messy, it will look less inviting to a potential thief.

TOP FIVE FESTIVALS FOR CAMPING

1. **Glastonbury** – The original camping and music festival. As you walk in and see the acres of tents sprawling into the horizon you know you're somewhere very special. You have to do it at least once.

2. **Fairport's Cropredy Convention** – If you like your folk electric, then this is the festival for you. Family friendly and definitely right on, this is the perfect way to introduce even young kids to the joys of music and outdoor living.

3. **Isle of Wight Festival** – With a laid-back vibe, stunning surrounds and a ferry to get you there, you'll believe you've gone somewhere really exotic!

4. **The Wickerman Festival** – Scotland's answer to America's Burning Man: music, tents and giant wicker statues. Just a normal Saturday night then...

5. **Wakestock** – Celebrating all things watery and musical – combining live bands with water sports contests and displays – nowhere in Europe does it as well as this gathering in North Wales, so pack your tent and your wetsuit for a festival that is seriously hot.

FESTIVAL SURVIVAL KIT

Whatever you do, don't leave home without...

- Toothbrush and toothpaste
- Earplugs
- Hand sanitiser
- Torch
- Tissues
- Rain poncho/waterproof jacket
- Wet wipes (the festival camper's shower)
- Sunscreen
- Mints
- First-aid kit

iPod Must-haves

Upload these songs to get you in the festival mood:

'Staying Out for the Summer' – Dodgy
'No Rain' – Blind Melon
'Beautiful Day' – U2
'Tents Along the Water' – Skygreen Leopards
'Light My Fire' – The Doors
'Call of the Wild' – Deep Purple

BEYOND THE TENT

These things, these 'recreational vehicles',
are like life-support systems on wheels.
Astronauts go to the moon with less backup.

BILL BRYSON, *THE LOST CONTINENT*, TALKING ABOUT RV CAMPERS

Tents are undoubtedly the cheapest, lightest and easiest way to head into the outdoors, but, for a bit of extra luxury, you can experience all the fun of camping in something altogether more sturdy, less damp and where you're virtually guaranteed a good night's sleep.

Campervans

A natural step for a lot of tent lovers, taking camping to the next level. Coming in a range of models and sizes – ranging from a glorified tent to recreation vehicles (RVs) that are nicer than flats some of us have rented – campervans are a great option for those who still want the sense of adventure that heading into the unknown can give, but with the assurance of a solid roof and lockable doors. Some buy one, others merely rent one for a week, but with the option to pull over and dine or sleep with a view out to sea or surrounded by mountains, it's easy to see the appeal.

CARAVANS

Static or moveable, is the question. Moveable means you are as flexible as with a campervan, with the added advantage of leaving your sleeping quarters somewhere picturesque while you nip to the supermarket in your car, or go for a day trip. Static ones mean when you find the perfect site you can make it a more permanent holiday home to visit, and they do tend to be the more luxurious models, as they don't need to focus on space saving in quite the same way as the ones you tow.

TRAILER TENTS

The solution for campers who can't quite make up their minds whether they want a caravan or a canvas model. There are obviously different designs, but they commonly look like a caravan with the top two thirds cut off and replaced with a tent. They provide a sturdy structure and have the advantage of raising your sleeping quarters well away from the ground – often on proper slatted bed frames which, some may argue, give a better night's sleep. They are easier to tow than a caravan, due to their smaller size, but the emphasis on these is that they are clearly a temporary structure and need to be stored carefully when not used.

YOU KNOW YOU'RE DONE WITH TENT CAMPING WHEN...

... you spend hours trying to find where you left the keys to your tent.

VW TRANSPORTER (1962) CAMPERVAN

Perhaps unreliable, maybe a tad rusty, but these nostalgic little vehicles have won a special place in many a camper's heart – especially this split-screen model. From its friendly, large VW logo on the front to its curves, chrome trims and quirky design, it's still one of the most sought-after campervans – despite the development of much more practical models. A recent incarnation of the VW Transporter has tried to win aficionados' hearts by promising some of the same features but with a much more modern twist, but for some, the 1962 is the defining model that no amount of new-fangled technology can top. Long live the Transporter – happy camping!

Top Five Campsites Where Tents Aren't Required

1. La Rosa, Whitby, North Yorkshire

01947 606981; http://larosa.co.uk

A chance to sleep in a retro vintage caravan decorated inside to reflect the era it's from – kitsch at its best!

2. Livingstone Lodge, Hythe, Kent

0844 842 4647; www.aspinallfoundation.org

Replica African safari tents await intrepid travellers to this venue within the Port Lympne Wild Animal & Safari Park and, better yet, some animals to gawp at, including a rhino and giraffe.

3. Gypsy Caravan, Black Mountains, Monmouthshire

0844 5005 101; www.underthethatch.co.uk

Snuggle up in a traditional Romany gypsy caravan on the edge of an idyllic river; one of the best reasons to leave the tent behind. The website takes bookings for a range of other romantic locations in Wales, England, Ireland, France and Portugal.

4. Sleeper Carriage, Glenfinnan, Scottish Highlands

01397 722295; www.glenfinnanstationmuseum.co.uk

Dream of the years when train travel was king in this converted carriage, situated within the grounds of the Glenfinnan Station Museum. Who needs a tent when you can sleep in this kind of luxury – buffet bar, anyone?

5. Mains Farm, Thornhill, Stirling

01786 850735; www.mainsfarmwigwams.com

Want a taste of the Wild West? Whether you fancy a night in a wooden wigwam or want to try your hand in a traditional tepee, you'll find both here.

BEFORE DITCHING THE TENT...

Feeling convinced that a campervan might soon replace your tent? There's a few things to bear in mind:

CAMPERVANNING

- Forget something? No problem, just get back behind the wheel and go get it.

- Feeling cold? You've got a heater on here, remember.

- You can buy cold food and know it will stay that way, courtesy of your fridge.

- Needing the loo won't mean rooting out the shovel, or even going outside.

CAMPING

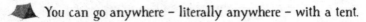 You can go anywhere – literally anywhere – with a tent.

You are far away from the roads and really, isn't that the reason you love camping in the first place?

You don't need to worry about locking doors, just zip and go.

Fresh air – you really can't beat it.

No smell from a toilet, because your waste is buried properly away from where you sleep (or in a toilet block).

It is, quite simply, better!

RESOURCES

Useful websites, organisations and publications for all your camping needs...

WEBSITES:

www.ukcampsite.co.uk

A great resource to find the best campsite for you with contacts, up-to-date information and reviews.

www.pitchup.com

Listings of many campsites all over the UK with honest reviews from real campers.

www.coolcamping.co.uk

Trendy, quirky and downright lovely campsites around the country with contact details and reviews.

http://goglamping.net

A directory where you can book to stay in a yurt, safari tent, tepee and many other types of luxurious glamping accommodation.

PUBLICATIONS:

Trail – the UK's best-selling hillwalking and outdoors magazine

Country Walking – magazine with walks of interest and monthly inspiration

Camping – magazine covering everything from tent camping to cool campsites and caravanning

ORGANISATIONS:

The Camping and Caravanning Club

www.campingandcaravanningclub.co.uk

The longest running camping club in the country. Membership gives you discounts on campsite fees, special offers and a special members' magazine.

Ramblers

www.ramblers.org.uk

From local walking groups to worldwide walking holidays, you're bound to meet some fellow tent-lovers here.

Mountain Bothies Association (MBA)

www.mountainbothies.org.uk

For those who fancy ditching the canvas for a night and spending time in a 'stone tent'. A small fee each year helps this volunteer-run group maintain the mountain shelters for us all to enjoy.

www.summersdale.com
@summersdale